SHERLOCK HOLMES'

Cunning Puzzles

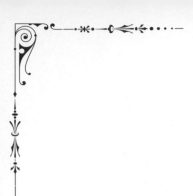

THIS IS A CARLTON BOOK

Published by Carlton Books Ltd
20 Mortimer Street
London W1T 3JW

A CIP catalogue for this book is available from the British Library.

ISBN 978-1-78097-962-5

Text and puzzles: Tim Dedopulos

The publishers would like to thank Mary Evans Picture Library for their
kind permission to reproduce the pictures in this book.

Every effort has been made to acknowledge correctly and contact the source
and/or copyright holder of each picture and Carlton Books Limited apologizes
for any unintentional errors or omissions, which will be corrected in future
editions of this book.

Content previously published as *The Sherlock Holmes Puzzle Collection: The Lost Cases*.

Printed in Dubai

SHERLOCK HOLMES'

Cunning Puzzles

Riddles, enigmas and challenges inspired
by the world's greatest crime-solver

Dr John Watson

CARLTON
BOOKS

Contents

Cunning

	Question	Answer
The Seven	76	133
Bridge	77	133
The Second Camouflage	78	134
The Ribbons	79	134
Billy and Jonny	80	135
Trout	81	135
Getting to Market	82	136
The Fifth Wordknot	84	137
Pencils	85	137
Two Wrongs	86	138
Easter Spirit	87	138
Three Men	88	139
Rufus	90	140
Manual	91	140
The Tyrant	92	141
Terminus	94	142
The Final Camouflage	95	142
Seven Applewomen	96	143

INTRODUCTION

The name of my dear friend and companion Mr Sherlock Holmes is familiar to all who possess any interest whatsoever in the field of criminal investigation. Indeed, there are some weeks where it hardly seems possible to pick up a newspaper without seeing his name splashed luridly across the front page. Unlike so many, however, his renown is justly deserved – not for nothing has he frequently been heralded as England's greatest detective, living or dead. Personally, I suspect that his abilities are unmatched anywhere in the world at this time.

I myself have been fortunate enough to share in Holmes' extraordinary adventures, and if I have been unable to rival his insight, I have consoled myself by acting as his de facto chronicler. I also flatter myself a little with the notion that I have, betimes, provided some little warmth of human companionship. We have spent many years, on and off, sharing rooms at 221b Baker Street, and I like to think that the experience has enriched both our existences. My name, though it is of little matter, is John Watson, and I am by profession a doctor.

My dear friend has long had a passionate ambition to improve the minds of humanity. He has often talked about writing a book that will help to instil the habits which he considers so absolutely vital to the art of deduction. Such a tome would be a revolutionary step in the history of mankind, and would most certainly address observation, logical analysis, criminal behaviour, scientific and mathematical knowledge, clear thinking, and much more besides. Alas, it has yet to materialize, for the world is full of villainy, and Sherlock Holmes is ever drawn to the solution of very real problems.

But over the course of our adventures, Holmes has never given up on the cause of improving my modest faculties. On innumerable occasions, he has presented me with opportunities to engage my mind, and solve some problem or other which to him is perfectly clear from the information already available. These trials have sometimes been quite taxing, and have not always come at a welcome moment, but I have engaged in all of them to the very best of my abilities. To do otherwise would be to dishonour the very generous gift my friend is making me in devoting time to my analytical improvement.

In truth, I do believe that his ministrations have indeed helped. I consider myself to be more aware than I was in my youth, and less prone to hasty assessments and faulty conclusions. If I have gained any greater talent in these areas, it is entirely thanks to the efforts that my friend has exerted on my behalf, for it is most certainly not an area for which I am naturally disposed. Give me a sickly patient, and I feel absolutely confident of swiftly arriving at the appropriate diagnosis and, to the limits provided by medical science, of attaining a successful recovery for the

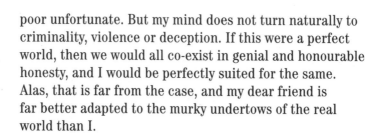

poor unfortunate. But my mind does not turn naturally to criminality, violence or deception. If this were a perfect world, then we would all co-exist in genial and honourable honesty, and I would be perfectly suited for the same. Alas, that is far from the case, and my dear friend is far better adapted to the murky undertows of the real world than I.

Still, as I have already attested, Holmes' little trials have had a beneficial effect even on me. For one who is more readily disposed to such efforts, the results may well be commensurately powerful. Thus, I have taken the liberty of assembling this collection.

Working assiduously from my notes, I have compiled somewhere in the region of 150 of the puzzles that Holmes has set me over the years. I have been assiduous in ensuring that I have described the situation as I first encountered it, with all pertinent information reproduced. The answers are as detailed as I can usefully make them. Some I managed to answer successfully myself; for others, I have reproduced Holmes' explanations as accurately as my notes permit.

To improve the accessibility a little, I have attempted to order the trials into approximate groupings of difficulty – fiendish and cunning, to be exact. Holmes has a devious mind, and there were times when he was entirely determined to baffle me, whilst on other occasions, the problems were simple enough to serve as illustrative examples of certain principles. I believe that I have broadly succeeded in classifying the difficulty of his riddles, but I beg your indulgence in so uncertain a matter. Every question is easy, if you know the answer, and the opposite holds equally true.

It is my fervent hope that you will find this little volume enlightening and amusingly diverting. If it may prove to sharpen your deductive sense a little, that would be all the vindication that I could ever possibly wish; all the credit for such improvement would be due Holmes himself. I, as always, am content to be just the scribe. I have taken every effort to ensure that the problems are all amenable to fair solution, but if by some remote happenchance that should prove not the case, it must be clear that the blame lies entirely on my shoulders, and that none should devolve to my dear companion.

My friends, it is with very real pleasure that I present to you this volume of the puzzles of Mr Sherlock Holmes.

I remain, as always, your servant,

Dr John H. Watson.

FIENDISH

PUZZLES

"You see, but you do not observe. The distinction is clear."

Sherlock Holmes

THE WEIGHTS

Mrs Hudson paused in the doorway to our rooms. "My cousin Amy's youngest turned three yesterday," she declared.

"Oh, congratulations," I said. Even as I said it, it occurred to me that it was a slightly fatuous comment.

"Thank you," she replied. "To mark the occasion, Amy and her husband Ben decided to measure the youngster's weight. They managed to find a public weighing machine, but from then on, things became somewhat troublesome. The family dog, Rebel, was with them, and true to his name he refused to take the matter seriously. In the end, the best that Amy could do was to get both child and husband weighed together with the dog, for a grand total of 180 lb."

"An impressive weight for a three-year-old," I observed.

"Yes, well, I was able to ascertain from Amy that Ben and the child together outweighed Rebel by 162 lb, and that the dog weighed just 30 per cent of the child's weight."

What is the weight of the child?

SOLUTION ON PAGE **100**

SOLARIS

Holmes has never been especially interested in matters astronomical. He maintains – and not without a certain justification, I suppose – that the revolutions of the heavenly bodies have very little impact on the solving of crimes. He knows the moon's phases, and is aware of upcoming eclipses, but otherwise maintains that he cares little for which astronomical body moves around which, or how swiftly.

Whilst I empathize with his focus, I feel a little differently. We live in a magnificent universe, and it seems a shame to me to not pay at least a little attention to its wonders. There is little so awe-inspiring, to my mind, as gazing up at a sky full of uncountable stars, knowing that any of them might be home to a planet with an intelligent being looking in my direction.

You know, I trust, that the Earth revolves upon its axis once per day – that being how the day is formed – as well as rotating entirely around the Sun once a year, in a counterclockwise direction. So my question is this: Does your speed of rotation (in relation to the Sun) change during the day, and if so, at what time are you moving the fastest?

SOLUTION ON PAGE  100

A WORSHIP OF WRITERS

During *The Adventure of the Third Carriage*, we found ourselves attempting to unravel the specific details of a collection of writers who came by train into London. The six of them entirely filled one compartment of the carriage, seated as they were in two rows of three, facing each other.

The facts that we managed to glean from the ticket inspector and other passers-by are these. The six men were called Tomkins, Archer, Squires, Whitely, Appleby and Gardner. Between them, their specialities covered short stories, histories, humour, novels, plays and poetry, and each was reading the latest work of one of the others in the carriage.

Squires was reading a work by the person sitting opposite him. Tomkins, who is not the historian, was reading a volume of short stories. Archer, the novelist's brother-in-law, was sitting between the humorist and the short-story writer, who, in turn, was opposite the historian. Whitely was reading a play and sitting opposite the novelist. Appleby, reading the humorous book, was next to the playwright. Tomkins was sitting in a corner. Gardner, finally, hated poetry.

Who was the novelist?

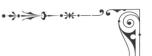

SOLUTION ON PAGE 101

LOGGERS

In Sussex, Holmes and I ran into a pair of woodcutters named Doug and Dave. There was an air of the unreliable about them – not helped by a clearly discernible aroma of scrumpy – but they nevertheless proved extremely helpful in guiding us to a particular hilltop clearing some distance outside of the town of Arundel. A shadowy group had been counterfeiting sorceries of a positively medieval kind, and all sorts of nastiness had ensued.

The Adventure of the Black Alchemist is not one that I would feel comfortable recounting, and if my life never drags me back to Chanctonbury Ring I shall be a happy man. But there is still some instructive material here. Whilst we were ascending our hill, Doug and Dave made conversation by telling us about their trade. According to these worthies, working together they were able to saw 600 cubic feet of wood into large logs over the course of a day, or split as much as 900 cubic feet of logs into chunks of firewood.

Holmes immediately suggested that they saw as much wood in the first part of the day as they would need in order to finish splitting it at the end of the day. It naturally fell to me to calculate precisely how much wood that would be.

Can you find the answer?

SOLUTION ON PAGE  102

THE FIRST WORDKNOT

I was in a tailor's shop on Jermyn Street when Holmes sprang his first wordknot upon me. In fact, I was being fitted for a jacket, and the tailor was most strict that I withhold from moving. It certainly made it harder to concentrate, and not having access to a pencil didn't help one bit, I can assure you. I wasn't even able to take the slip of paper, which Holmes cheerfully held out in front of me for reference.

I impose no such unreasonable strictures upon you.

The slip of paper bore ten rows of three letters, each one containing one letter, in normal sequence, of a ten-letter word. The letters in each row were in no particular order, however, making the task of unscrambling the three loosely themed words quite challenging.

The rows were as follows:

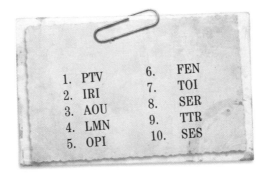

1. PTV
2. IRI
3. AOU
4. LMN
5. OPI
6. FEN
7. TOI
8. SER
9. TTR
10. SES

Can you find the words?

SOLUTION ON PAGE 102

TWO SUMS

Holmes took a sip of tea. "Fancy an abstract challenge, Watson?"

To be entirely honest, that sort of question tended to fill me with a formless dread. But, knowing it was undoubtedly a useful exercise, I replied that I was prepared to give it a try.

"Excellent," he replied. "Take the digits from 1 to 9, specifically omitting 6. That gives you eight digits. Group those into numbers of your choice – say 1, 23, 457, 8 and 9, for example – in such a way that you can divide these into two sets of numbers, each containing four digits. In our example's case, that could be 1 and 457, and 23, 8 and 9. The trick is to have the sum of your two sets of numbers be the same. 1 + 457 clearly does not equal 23 + 8 + 9." He paused, while my brain reeled a little. "Before you ask, no, you are not allowed to rotate the 9 to turn it into a 6."

"Such a thought never occurred to me," I protested.

"No? Ah well"

Can you find the solution?

SOLUTION ON PAGE 103

DUCK DUCK GOOSE

*T**he Peculiar Case of the Raven Child* took Holmes and I to the Dysynni Valley. Whilst much of what we encountered there was odd to say the least, there was at least a horrible logic to it, at least when examined after the fact.

The same could not be said of a sign we saw outside one farmer's cottage. "Two chickens for a duck; three chickens and a duck for two geese," it declared, in wild handwriting. In smaller, neater lettering beneath, there was a further offer: "Three geese, one chicken and two ducks for 25 shillings. NO CHANGE".

"Eccentric fellow," I observed to Holmes.

"Probably spent the night alone on the top of Cader Idris," he replied. "Still, there's enough information there to work out the price of a duck, if you assume his 'no change' means that each bird costs a whole number of shillings."

Can you work out the value of a duck?

THE JEWELLER

During *The Adventure of the Impossible Gecko*, we had reason to examine the movements of a certain jeweller of Hatton Garden, a fellow named Stewartson. The Baker Street Irregulars were despatched to keep an eye on his movements, particularly with regards to the timing of his journey to and from work.

When Wiggins reported back to us, he informed us that Stewartson often took a hansom cab to and from work, and on those occasions, his total journey time to and from his shop was 30 minutes. On some mornings, however, he walked into work, and then caught a cab home when he finished. On those occasions, his total journey time was one and a half hours.

I made some comment to the effect that Wiggins could just have told us how long it took the fellow to walk to work, and Holmes archly replied that he'd done just that.

How long was Stewartson's walk to work?

SOLUTION ON PAGE 104

THE NOTE

Holmes had been tinkering away in his study for the best part of a couple of hours, testing a range of pungent chemical experiments, when he came out bearing a purple-speckled notebook.

"Take a look at this, old chap," he said, and passed it over.

I took the notebook, and was about to examine it when Holmes turned on his heel and returned to the study. "Let me know when you've cracked it," he said, before closing the door.

Mystified, I opened the book, trying to avoid the purple splotches. The front page was the only one to bear any writing, and its contents were these:

What should the next line be?

SOLUTION ON PAGE  105

SERPENTINE

olmes and I were sitting in Hyde Park on a pleasant Sunday afternoon, watching people boating on the river. Specifically, we were watching Alice Mills and her beau, Gabriel Sieger. Thus far, Miss Mills had done nothing particularly noteworthy, but it was a reasonably diverting way of spending an afternoon.

"You know, I assume, that a boat, floating, displaces a certain amount of water," Holmes said, conversationally.

I nodded.

"You also know, I trust, that the weight of the water displaced is equal to the weight of the boat."

I nodded again, wondering where he was going.

"It follows then that Miss Mills and Mr Sieger together will have raised the level of the water a small amount when they got into the boat, which we can assume was already afloat."

"I suppose so," I said.

"So what would happen to the level of the water if Mr Sieger fell out of the boat, and those counterfeiter's plates in his jacket sank him to the floor of the Serpentine like a stone?"

SOLUTION ON PAGE  105

THE LEGACY

I remember reading in the *Evening Standard* of an instance where an old soldier died childless, and left his modest bequest to his nephews, Ronald and Frederick. It was just below a silly story about a Canadian poltergeist. The piece was of interest only because of the somewhat tangled way in which the deceased had specified the money be divided. The newspaper took a humorous slant on the story, playing up the perplexity of the lawyer involved, and painting the dead man as an enthusiastic prankster. The truth of these claims is left to your personal judgement regarding the veracity of newspaper reporters.

However editorialized the story might have been, the base facts were that the fellow left £100 precisely, and determined the allotment of inheritance by saying that subtracting a third of Ronald's legacy from a quarter of Frederick's would give a difference of £11.

How much did Ronald get?

SOLUTION ON PAGE  106

CHILDREN

Having brought up some breakfast for Holmes and myself, Mrs Hudson rather spoilt my appetite by informing us that her cousin Davey and his wife were trying vigorously for a family. Whilst I was still attempting to get rid of the mental images thus conjured, she continued by saying, "They've decided they'd like to have four children, nice and quickly."

As a doctor, I naturally found the idea of both "nice" and "quickly" being applied to four pregnancies to be somewhat implausible, but I held my peace.

Mrs Hudson continued blithely on. "They're hoping not to get all four children the same sex. The real question, of course, is whether they're more likely to have two of each, or three of one."

"I'm sure the good Doctor could answer that for you," Holmes said, arching an eyebrow in my direction. "Assuming they're equally likely to have a boy or a girl each time."

"Oh, yes," said Mrs Hudson. "Thank you, Doctor." I'm sure I saw her suppressing a mischievous grin.

Can you work out the answer?

SOLUTION ON PAGE 107

THE REVENGE

Edward Blaydon was the captain of the *Revenge*, an ill-aspected sloop that claimed Cape Town as its home berth. This was during *The Adventure of the Sapphire Gin*, and a very strange affair it was too. Holmes had lured Blaydon to a luncheon in St. James's, where we met him in the guise of shady exporters to ostensibly discuss the transport of a cargo from Whitby to Varna, on the Bulgarian coast.

"I know the Black Sea like the back of my hand," Blaydon said confidently. "I can get your merchandise into Varna, no questions asked, and that's a guarantee. I'll do it in under a week, too."

"That sounds very promising," Holmes replied. "Are you certain that your ship is up to the task?"

"The *Revenge*? Ha! Of course. I admit that it's not much to look at, but it's one of the fastest packet-runners you'll find in any of London's docks."

Holmes nodded thoughtfully. "I noticed that you're registered in Cape Town. Is that where you're from?"

"Where's any seaman from, Mr Gordon?" "Gordon" was Holmes. I was going by "Hendricks". "I belong to the oceans. Ports are just places where you buy booze, food, and other little niceties. I'm a Portsmouth lad, originally. But I've spent my time in the shadow of Table Mountain, if that's what's worrying you."

A little while later, we took our leave with some vague promises and assurances. As soon as we were out of the restaurant, Holmes shook his head disapprovingly. "I assume that you realized our friend was no sailor, Watson? Anyone hearing him would have."

What did he mean?

SOLUTION ON PAGE 108

THE TRUNK

Holmes and I were walking along a sleepy lane in Hookland, making our way back to the inn at which we had secured lodgings after scouting out the estates of the supposed major, C. L. Nolan. Up ahead, a tractor was slowly pulling a chained tree trunk along the lane. Fortunately it had been trimmed of its branches, but it was still an imposing sight.

When we'd overtaken the thing, Holmes surprised me by turning sharply on his heel and walking back along the trunk. I stopped where I was to watch him. He continued at a steady pace until he'd passed the last of it, then reversed himself once more, and walked back to me.

"Come along, old chap," he said as he walked past.

Shaking my head, I duly followed.

"It took me 140 paces to walk from the back of the tree to the front, and just 20 to walk from the front to the back," he declared.

"Well of course," I said. "The tree was moving, after all."

"Precisely," he said. "My pace is one yard in length, so how long is that tree-trunk?"

Can you find the answer?

SOLUTION ON PAGE 108

THE FIELD

One of the side effects of our trip to Hookland was that for several days thereafter, Holmes was given to couching his little mental exercises for me in agricultural terms. I suppose it did make something of a change to be considering matters pastoral rather than, say, fiscal or horological. There was something a little odd about it, however. Either way, it came to an end when *The Adventure of the Wandering Bishops* did.

As a practical example, consider this problem that Holmes set me during that period. There is a particular field which three of a farmer's animals – a cow, a goat, and a lamb – are set to graze. If it were just the cow and the goat, they would graze it bare in 45 days. Without the cow, the goat and the lamb will consume all the grass in 90 days. Absent the goat, the cow and lamb will eat all the pasture in 60 days. The farmer, however, has turned all three loose in the field. How long will it take the three combined to graze out the field?

You may assume for the sake of simplicity that the growth of the grass is irrelevant.

SOLUTION ON PAGE 109

g .

THE TYPE

During *The Adventure of the Third Carriage*, we spent some time talking to a printer. Holmes was after some nugget of information, but felt that the matter needed to be addressed obliquely, so we spent more than an hour with the fellow.

He was nice enough, as printers go, but he was somewhat fixated on a batch of calendars that had been commissioned from him. They were of the style of one month to a page, and had to be printed in a very specific – and expensively ornate – typeface. Because of this, the man was keen to minimize the number of movable-type letters that he had to purchase.

He was quite proud of himself for having found the thriftiest solution that would allow him to print the names of the months in full. Using all capital letters was part of it, of course, but the main portion involved ensuring that he had just enough individual letters to assemble any given month.

Can you work out how many letters he had to purchase?

SOLUTION ON PAGE
109

THE STABBING

"It was the butler who found my father on the floor of the study, Mr Holmes." Emma Porter was a pleasant-seeming woman in her late twenties, her face heavily scored with grief. "He actually stumbled over the body in the darkness. The fire had gone out, you see. His shrieks woke the maid and myself up."

"Did you have any reason to suspect your father was in danger?" Holmes kept his voice politely neutral in tone.

"No, of course not. I mean, he had to lay a fellow off yesterday, and he had a rival or two, but who would stoop to brutal murder over chauffeuring?" Her eyes welled with tears.

"Why did he sack that chap?"

"Drinking," she said. "At least, that's what I understood."

Holmes frowned slightly. "Did he ever drive clients himself?"

"Almost never, but perhaps if he was short-staffed he might have. He generally kept himself distant from the drivers."

"I see," Holmes said. "And he was found dead shortly after midnight."

"That's right," she said. "The butler was on his way to bed, but noticed that Father was on the floor as he passed the study. I had been asleep for some hours by that point. The maid would have been in bed by 11, too. All the windows were closed, of course. The police said that he'd been stabbed repeatedly. It just doesn't make sense." She folded inward on herself gently.

"I'm confident we'll find the answers very soon," Holmes said. "We already have our primary suspect."

Who does Holmes suspect, and why?

SOLUTION ON PAGE  110

THE MANAGER

Once the safety of the frightened carpenter was assured, and the tome located to a reasonable degree of safety (if not actually recovered), Holmes and I had occasion to speak to a rather evasive little warehouse manager and his somewhat apologetic deputy. The deputy was clearly of better character, so whilst I distracted the manager with some discussion of high-grade medical steel, Holmes chatted to the younger man.

───────

Later, as we departed, Holmes told me a curious thing. The deputy, he said, confessed to him that he had actually enquired about his boss's age a few days beforehand. He was told that the manager was twice as old as the deputy had been, back when the manager had been the same age as the deputy now was.

We already knew from our researches that the manager was 48. How old did that make the deputy?

SOLUTION ON PAGE  110

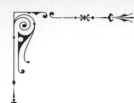
BALANCE

One morning, I observed Holmes rolling a shilling back and forth over his knuckles, from one finger to the next, with his other hand held behind his back. "You can do a lot of mischief with a tricked coin, old friend," he said.

"That looks real enough to me," I replied.

"This? Oh, it is. But surely you have heard of gamblers' coins that are cunningly weighted to favour heads over tails, or vice versa?"

I allowed that I had indeed.

"Such devices are a nasty trap for the unwary. But it is possible to get a totally unbiased either/or result from any weighted coin."

"Oh?"

"Indeed. Can you tell me how?"

Can you work it out?

SOLUTION ON PAGE **111**

GETTING AHEAD

F licking through a book on European history, I came across a rather odd account, which I shared with Holmes.

———◆———

"According to this text, which I admit is somewhat sensationalized, during the French Revolution, the locals of Nîmes used to wager on the sizes of the severed heads of nobles and other supposed enemies of the Revolution. The task was to estimate how large the head would be once it had been dipped in wax, but before it had been set out for display. People would bring along vegetables, sometimes carefully trimmed, which they felt would best match the head of a particular condemned person. The closest guess won the pot."

"Ingenious and enterprising," Holmes replied. "Thoroughly French."

"It seems like the very devil of a thing to judge," I said.

"Really?" Holmes sounded amused. "Can you not think of a simple way to get a precise verdict?"

SOLUTION ON PAGE  111

BICYCLE

I noticed Holmes looking distracted one morning over breakfast, tossing a piece of toast into the air before catching it again, over and over like a cat with a toy.

"Something on your mind, old man?" I asked him.

"The valencies of sulphur," he replied. "Particularly in the way that they relate to its propensity to form astringents with zinc."

"Ah," I replied.

"Here's something mostly unrelated for you to chew over, my dear Watson. Say you and I have a single bicycle between us, and no other transport options save walking. We want to get the both of us to a location 18 miles distant as swiftly as possible. If my walking speed is five miles per hour compared to your four, but for some reason – perhaps a bad ligament – my cycling speed is eight miles per hour compared to your ten, how would you get us simultaneously to our destination with maximum rapidity?"

"A cab," I suggested.

"Without cheating," Holmes replied, and went back to tossing his toast in the air.

SOLUTION ON PAGE 112

THE CANVAS

"Let us say that I needed to paint a very particular picture," Holmes said to me one afternoon.

"I would find such a proposition alarming, given your utter absence of any previously displayed artistic talent," I said.

"You do me a disservice," Holmes replied. "But that is not important. This painting needs to occupy precisely 72 square inches, and measure a whole number of inches on each side. Furthermore, it needs to have a clear border of exactly four inches above and below, and two inches to either side."

"That is quite specific," I observed.

"Very much so," he said. "What is the smallest canvas I could fit such a painting on?"

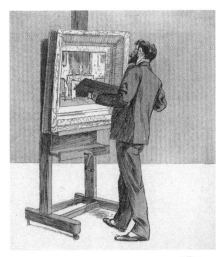

SOLUTION ON PAGE 112

PIG

I n Hookland, Holmes and I discovered that the elusive C. L. Nolan had made a suspiciously large purchase of livestock. Converting all the assorted value to shillings for simplicity, he bought pigs at 95s each, and sheep at 97s each, for a grand total of 4,238s – well over 200 pounds sterling. The dealer who furnished us with this information was still somewhat dazed by the entire transaction. About the only other pieces of information that we got out of the fellow were that Nolan paid entirely in crown coins of all things, and that he would somehow arrange for the livestock to be transported to a number of destinations over the next few weeks.

It was very peculiar, which honestly rather matches my overall opinion of Hookland as a county.

As we left the dealer, Holmes said to me, "So how many pigs did he purchase?"

It was late that night before I could furnish him with an answer. Can you find one?

SOLUTION ON PAGE 113

THE SECOND WORDKNOT

Ireceived my second slip of wordknot paper from Holmes as we were bouncing down the horribly uneven streets of Bethnal Green in a cab. At the time, it seemed all too plausible that the driver's mind had been seized by fiends or, at the very least, some esoteric specimen of mental disturbance. Holmes had clearly been waiting for precisely such an occasion, for he whipped out the note with a delighted flourish, and presented it to me.

I received it with lamentable ill grace. On it were the usual ten lines of three jumbled letters, each row being formed by taking one letter from each of three ten-letter words, starting with the three initial letters on the first row, and proceeding regularly to the ten final letters on the tenth row. The task of unpicking the three loosely themed ten-letter words was not helped by my ongoing fear of imminent disaster, nor by my fight to prevent my breakfast from attempting escape.

The rows of letters were as follows:

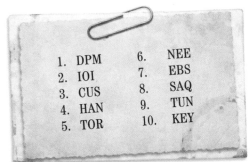

1. DPM
2. IOI
3. CUS
4. HAN
5. TOR
6. NEE
7. EBS
8. SAQ
9. TUN
10. KEY

Can you find the words?

SOLUTION ON PAGE 114

THE SHOPKEEPER

Whilst browsing in a shop one dreary afternoon, I overheard the following conversation taking place between a shopkeeper and a neatly dressed gentleman of advancing years. At the time, it made perfect sense, but on reflection, it occurs to me that it might be an amusing test.

"What would it cost me for just one?" the gentleman asked.

"Two shillings," came the reply.

The customer nodded. "So that means 12 would cost...?"

"Four shillings," the shopkeeper said, keeping his voice carefully patient.

"That's very good," the customer replied. "I'll take 312 then, please."

"Of course, sir." The shopkeeper started collecting items for the customer. "Six shillings, please."

What was the gentleman purchasing?

SOLUTION ON PAGE 114

MATCH TWO

A s Holmes put it when setting me this challenge, "You may find that a bit of mechanical aid proves of assistance with this one, my dear Watson." In other words, get some toothpicks or matches.

The task is, using matches, to remove seven-tenths of five and in so doing, leave exactly four remaining.

It is quite obvious when you know how it is done, but to be frank, I did struggle for a while with this one. Holmes was quite steadfast in refusing me any sort of hint, and merely sat there, poring through a rather sensationalist volume of criminal activity that had taken place in Leeds over the past few years. From what little I saw of it, it must have been depressing reading. Not, of course, that I should wish to give the impression that I am singling Leeds out as especially criminal; merely that Holmes' interest in crime was entirely catholic.

Anyhow, Leeds is by the by. Can you find the solution?

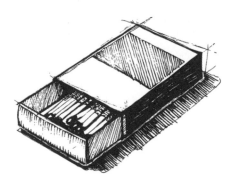

SOLUTION ON PAGE (115)

CURIO

"I have a little mathematical curio for you," Holmes told me one afternoon.

I eyed him warily. "Oh?"

"There are two separate pairs of numbers between one and nine which, when each is squared, and these squares are added to the product of multiplying the numbers together, give you a total which is also a square. Can you identify one of the pairs?"

"Let me just straighten that out," I told him. "Two different single-digit numbers, no zeroes. Multiply them by each other, and by themselves. Add the three totals together, and get a square number. Find one of two solutions."

"Precisely so," Holmes said. "There are only 81 pairs, if you don't fancy tackling the algebra."

Can you solve the problem?

SOLUTION ON PAGE 115

SIX FEET UNDER

Holmes and I were walking across the Regent's Park on our way back to 221b, having just sorted out the unpleasant *Affair of the Maida Vale Baker*. It was 13 June, a date which sticks in my mind for reasons that will swiftly become quite clear. We were just passing the nursery when Holmes glanced over at the blooming flowerbeds, and bade me stop. I did so immediately, alert for any sign of pursuit.

"We're almost to the longest day of the year," he proclaimed. "We sit on the very cusp of spring and summer. Agreed?"

I nodded, mildly bemused.

"So tell me then, Watson. What season is it, ten feet straight down?"

SOLUTION ON PAGE **116**

ENGINE TROUBLE

I t is a long haul from Bangor to London by train, particularly when your route requires several changes. The Dysynni Valley is beautiful, in a stark sense, but it's a devil of a haul from Baker Street. Our journey back was not helped by an engine problem that one of the trains on our route developed.

We'd been on this particular leg of the journey for an hour when our speed was suddenly cut to three-fifths of its former magnitude. Consequently, we were two hours late arriving at our destination, and missed our connection.

The guard did apologize on behalf of the driver, and informed us that if the problem had developed 50 miles later, we would have arrived 40 minutes sooner, and made our connection. This was not any great comfort.

Can you calculate how long this particular leg of the journey was?

SOLUTION ON PAGE 116

RECALL

Memory is a curious thing. I recall a conversation with Holmes on the matter, where he proposed that there were in fact many different forms of memory – immediate, autobiographical, muscular, visual, audial, linguistic, and more – and that different people would often have varied facilities in these areas. Certainly, I knew a fellow with a very sharp memory, who could recall a snatch of song or read a passage from a decade ago with perfect alacrity, but had genuine trouble recalling what he'd done the day before, and had to work his birthday out by starting with the current date.

At the conclusion of the discussion, Holmes proceeded to test my immediate memory with a rather confusing little mental calculation.

"Tell me," he said, "what is the number which when tripled, and this product increased by 75 per cent, the result divided by seven, the quotient reduced by a third, the result multiplied by itself, this square reduced by 52, the square root found of this remaining difference, this root added to eight, and the sum divided by ten, results in the number two?"

Luckily, I have good short-term recall. You have the advantage of being able to refer back to the problem.

SOLUTION ON PAGE 117

MORAN

A s you may be aware, Holmes and I on occasion tangled with an extremely lethal fellow by the name of Colonel Moran. Holmes believed him to be the second most dangerous man in London at one time, and was almost certainly correct.

One of the incidents which led Moran to leave the army was a disagreement over a brutal firearm that he had personally invented. There was a call at the time for improved weapons, with a substantial purse waiting for those who could match the stringent requirements. Moran put forth a repeating rifle which, he said, would fire 60 shots at the rate of one every five seconds.

It is true that the assessing panel, who were men of good character, were ill-disposed to accept Moran's petition. Even then, he had the reputation of a brutal, nigh-uncontrollable monster. Still, they had technicians test the device. The panel accepted that Moran's gun took five minutes to fire 60 shots, and then rejected the rifle on the grounds that it did not live up to his claims. Moran was incandescent, and within six months had become a career criminal specializing in assassination and card-sharping.

Was the panel's assessment of failure accurate?

SOLUTION ON PAGE 117

THE MURDER OF MOLLY GLASS

The death of Molly Glass seemed like a tragic suicide. The woman in question, who was married and in her thirties, but childless, was found dead inside her bedroom. The room contained a gas fire, connected to the mains, as is so common nowadays. The gas was switched on, but unlit, and this was most definitely the cause of death. Post-mortem indicators made this perfectly plain. The windows of the bedroom were firmly closed, and latched from the inside. They were unbroken and undisturbed. The bedroom door was also locked from the inside, and there were no other means of egress.

Mrs Glass's mother was most insistent that her daughter would never have taken her own life, and refused to believe the police's complacent insistence on suicide. The lack of any sort of note did certainly encourage the possibility of such speculation. And so the case duly came before Holmes. He glanced at the details, and then tossed them aside, declaring that it was clearly murder, that her husband was mostly likely the culprit, and that his expertise was needed no further in the matter.

He was, of course, correct in all points. But how was it done?

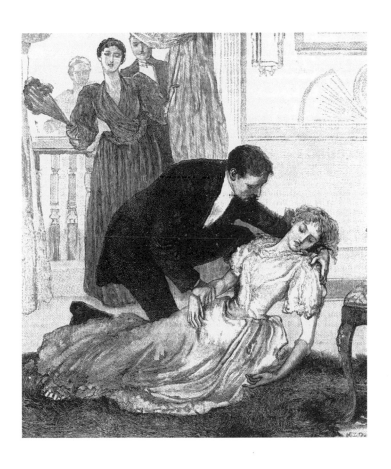

SOLUTION ON PAGE 118

THE THIRD WORDKNOT

You are probably familiar with Mr Joseph Paxton's glittering masterpiece, the Crystal Palace. Holmes and I were within its glass confines one afternoon. A fellow by the name of Andrew Hodder was going to be within the Alhambran Court, and for several reasons, Holmes felt it wise to observe him.

Mr Hodder duly arrived, and swiftly took a seat, then started sketching. After a minute or so, Holmes decided that Hodder was clearly going to be some time, and handed me the paper on which was recorded the third wordknot. As on previous occasions, this took the form of ten rows of three letters, thus:

1. HRH
2. EAO
3. SON
4. DDT
5. CWR
6. AIU
7. FIN
8. KNF
9. EEE
10. DDD

Three loosely related ten-letter words were obscured within, their first letters on the first row, their second letters on the second row, and so on. My task, which I hand down to you, was to unravel the three words.

Can you find the solution?

SOLUTION ON PAGE 119

BARNABAS

We met up with Wiggins one fine spring morning to find him in particularly high spirits. When we enquired, he explained that he'd helped an ageing gardener of his acquaintance to dig a client's ditch the afternoon before, for which he had been handsomely paid.

"He tried to give me three half-crowns," Wiggins said, sounding slightly awed. "Said it was what he'd be paid for the ditch, and as I'd done most of the work, and helped him out of a spot besides, I could take it all. I only took what was fair, though. Greed is bad for business, and this way maybe he'll have me help out some other time."

"Very admirable," I told him. "What was your fair share?"

Wiggins grinned, and winked at Holmes. "Thought you'd ask me that, Doctor. Look at it this way. Old Barnabas was able to dig as rapidly as I could shovel the loose dirt out of the trench, but I could dig four times as fast as he could shovel out dirt. It's not that either of us was worse at shovelling than at digging, you understand. It's just slower. The effort rate is the same. So you tell me, what do you think is fair?"

It took me a while to find an answer. Can you do so?

SOLUTION ON PAGE  **119**

CUNNING PUZZLES

"There is nothing like first-hand evidence."

Sherlock Holmes

THE FOURTY-FOUR

M rs Hudson seemed out of sorts. It was nothing that I could immediately put my finger on, but something was amiss.

I offered her a smile. "Are you feeling quite alright, Mrs Hudson?"

She sighed. "I'm fine, Doctor. Thank you. I'm concerned about my uncle Michael. I saw him on Sunday for the first time in several years. He lives down on the Lizard now, you know, in Cornwall. At one point the conversation turned to age, and I asked him how old my cousin Minnie was now. He fell silent for a moment, and then told me that she was 1,280 years old! Then he corrected himself, and said that she was 44. But her older brother Douglas was 40 last year. I got to the root of it in the end – he first multiplied her age with his own, and then subtracted hers from it. I'm afraid his mind is going."

"I'm dreadfully sorry to hear that," I told her. "It's a terrible business."

She thanked me, and carried on. After she'd left, I found myself pondering the ages of Minnie and her father. Can you work them out?

SOLUTION ON PAGE

122

PIPE DREAMS

W hilst I was serving in the army, I spent some time in Afghanistan, and there I came across a curious treatise that had been translated into English. The document, entitled *The Red Tower*, claimed to be the work of one Ghirgiz al-Uqbar, a name that suggested a non-local origin. It was a highly whimsical piece, but one section in particular is worth recalling for my current purposes.

In this section, the author decries the even population balance between men and women, suggesting that there ought to be more women, so that harems could be larger. From this highly dubious suggestion, he goes on to state that if he were ruler, he would pass an edict that required a woman to stop having children if and only if she had a son. Thus, he reasoned, families would have many daughters but just one son, and in a score of years, there would be a surfeit of unmarried young women.

His plan was clearly insane, but do you think it would have worked, if somehow implemented rigorously?

SOLUTION ON PAGE 123

THE OLD ONES

A curious incident in Bethnal Green came to my attention one Tuesday morning, in the *Evening Standard*. A fellow walked into a pub on the Cambridge Heath Road, and asked the man behind the bar for a glass of water. The response was immediate – the man pulled out a gun, and immediately shot the would-be customer dead.

Unfortunately for the murderer, there was a witness he was unaware of, one of the regular serving girls. She escaped detection, and was able to describe the day's horror to the police. She was also able to confirm that the murderer did not appear to have known the victim or harbour any sort of grudge against him, but also did not seem to be killing simply for the dark joy of it. According to the newspaper, the police even mentioned that the victim had not had hiccups.

Can you find the reason why this murder happened?

SOLUTION ON PAGE  124

RIFLE ROUNDS

Whilst in Afghanistan, I stumbled across the odd fact that rifle shells were packed in boxes of 15, 18 or 20 shells. This piqued my interest, so during a quiet moment, I sought out a quartermaster to enquire as to the reasoning behind it.

"It's so they can send out exactly as many shells as a dump needs without having to muck around with breaking open a box," the man told me.

"Surely that can't work," I said. "What if you wanted seven shells? Or 29?"

"What dump is ever going to want just seven shells?" replied the quartermaster. "Yes, alright, there are some low numbers where it breaks down, and you have to send more, but for the vast majority of orders, it's just fine. Anything over a certain threshold will work, you know."

Can you calculate what that threshold might be?

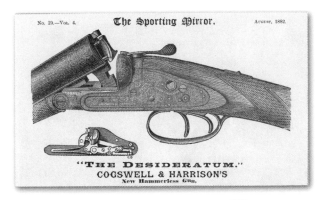

SOLUTION ON PAGE  124

THE PLEASANT WAY

During *The Peculiar Case of the Raven Child*, Holmes and I had cause to examine the movements of a suspicious fellow named Rowlands. I won't bore you with the specifics of the intrigue here, but one morning, Rowlands set out to walk over the hills from Tywyn to another town a modest distance away. At precisely the same time, his acquaintance Jones left Rowlands' destination, heading for Tywyn.

Their movements were notably suspicious. The pair met briefly at the point ten miles from Tywyn. Spending identical amounts of time in their destinations, they set off on their return journeys in such a manner that they met again, this time 12 miles from Jones' original starting point. Their walking speeds, of course, were consistent throughout.

How far apart are the two towns?

SOLUTION ON PAGE  125

FASHION

On one occasion, Holmes and I were asked to solve the robbery of a number of dresses from the workshop of a recently deceased ladies' tailor to the upper echelons of society. Holmes took a short look at the particulars of the case, and sent them all back to the gown-maker's son with a scribbled note to the effect that it could only be one particular seamstress, with the help of her husband.

However, glancing through my observations some period later, I observed certain facts about the robbery which led me to an interesting little exercise. The stock at the workshop had been very recently valued at the princely sum of £1,800, and when examined after the theft, comprised of precisely 100 completed dresses in a range of styles, but of equal valuation. However, there was no remaining record of how many dresses had been there beforehand. The son did recall his father stating, of the valuation, that if he'd had 30 dresses more, then a valuation of £1,800 would have meant £3 less per dress.

Are you able to calculate how many dresses were stolen?

SOLUTION ON PAGE  125

THE FIRST CAMOUFLAGE

I'd just scalded the roof of my mouth on a surprisingly hot spoonful of Scots porridge one morning when Holmes decided to seize the moment and throw one of his camouflaged word puzzles at me. The words he called out to me were stonecutter, tardigrades, cassowaries and matrimonial.

I knew from bitter experience that Holmes would not repeat the words, so made an effort to memorize them whilst simultaneously attempting to resist the urge to yell aloud at the pain in my mouth.

The task, as ever, was to discover the four smaller words, one within each of the longer, that were united by a common theme.

Can you do it? I recommend not burning yourself in the mouth before beginning. It is not helpful.

SOLUTION ON PAGE  126

THE APPLE MARKET

We stumbled across a practical instance of this odd little puzzler whilst in Hookland. Rather than try to replicate our experience exactly, however, I shall endeavour to abstract it slightly, so that it is easier to see to the heart of the matter. Hookland, as I have mentioned earlier, is a strange county.

The market held a group of three apple-sellers, friends with different species of apples to sell, and thus different prices. One of the ladies sold her apples at two for a penny, the second at three for a penny, and the third at five for tuppence. Around 11 a.m., however, the first two ladies had to suddenly depart. Each had 30 apples remaining. These 60 were handed to the remaining friend, who proceeded to sell them at her usual price of five for two pence.

If the two missing ladies had stayed to sell their stock, they would have brought in 25 pence between them. Now three apples at one penny and two apples at one penny together clearly equals five apples for tuppence. However, when the third lady sold her friends' stock, she brought in only 24 pence, as 60 divided by five is 12, and split that evenly between her friends.

So where did the odd penny get to?

SOLUTION ON PAGE (126)

A PAIR OF FOURS

Holmes took a puff on his pipe. "You are familiar, I trust, my dear Watson, with the principle of expressing a whole number in terms of a different number plus some mathematical operators."

I nodded. "Such as four being two times two, you mean."

"Precisely. And 63 being two to the power of two times two plus two, with two divided by two subtracted from it."

I jotted $(2^{\wedge}(2*2+2))$-2/2 down on a notepad, resolved it to $(2^{\wedge}6)$-1 = 64-1 = 63, and nodded again.

"Capital," Holmes said. "So can you likewise find a way of expressing 64 using as many mathematical operators as you like, but only two instances of the digit four, and no other digits? It may take you a little time."

SOLUTION ON PAGE  127

ASHCOURT STATION

As I know all too well, it takes five hours to get from Ashcourt to London Waterloo – or back, for that matter. Trains leave every hour, on the hour, in both directions. Holmes and I were on the Waterloo train, heading back to London with a certain amount of relief. Some time after our departure, a train rattled past in the other direction, heading into Ashcourt.

"More poor devils heading into Hookland," I observed.

"They're not the last we'll see," said Holmes absentmindedly.

"No," I said, although now I think about it, using a negative to indicate agreement does seem slightly farcical. Versatile language we have.

"In fact, Watson," Holmes said, "Why don't you tell me how many Waterloo-to-Ashcourt trains will pass us on our way?"

SOLUTION ON PAGE 127

OLD HOOK

An event that occurred during *The Adventure of the Wandering Bishops* inspired Holmes to devise a particularly tricky little mental exercise for my ongoing improvement. There were times when I thoroughly appreciated and enjoyed his efforts, and times when I found them somewhat unwelcome. I'm afraid this was one of the latter occasions. It had been a bad week.

"Picture three farmers," Holmes told me. "Hooklanders. We'll call them Ern, Ted, and Hob."

"If I must," I muttered.

"It will help," Holmes replied. "Ern has a horse and cart, with an average speed of eight mph. Ted can walk just one mph, given his bad knee, and Hob is a little better at two mph, thanks to his back."

"A fine shower," I said. "Can't I imagine them somewhat fitter?"

"Together, these worthies want to go from Old Hook to Coreham, a journey of 40 miles. So Ern got Ted in his cart, drove him most of the way, and dropped him off to walk the rest. Then he went back to get Hob, and took him into Coreham, arriving exactly as Ted did. How long did the journey take?"

Can you find a solution?

SOLUTION ON PAGE 128

ANDREW

Holmes and I have encountered many highly peculiar individuals over the years. One of the most singular, however, was a fellow by the name of Andrew, who was caught up in *The Adventure of the Black Alchemist*. Despite a certain preoccupation with fried-egg sandwiches, he was a quick-witted and resourceful fellow, and his heart was in the right place, both metaphorically and medically.

I vividly remember him explaining to Holmes and myself that he had lost his pocket watch in a scuffle with a cloaked and hooded figure whom he suspected of being an occultist. He went on to explain that on occasion when he forgot to wind his carriage clock at home, he would rectify the problem by visiting his friend David, who somehow always anticipated his arrival. Then he'd spend the evening there, and return home, correctly setting his clock when he arrived back.

It occurred to me that this must be rather haphazard, as he had no way of precisely telling the duration of the return trip, but he countered that as long as he took as long going there as he did getting back, it didn't matter.

What was his method?

SOLUTION ON PAGE 129

CENTURIAL

One afternoon, Mrs Hudson rather unexpectedly provided Holmes and myself with a slice of Victoria sponge cake each to go with our teas.

"Is it a special occasion, Mrs Hudson?" I enquired.

"Indeed it is, Doctor. Indeed it is."

I smiled. "Oh, well –"

"Yes, my cousin Jack and his sons total precisely 100 years of age between them today," she said proudly. "Further more, Jack is exactly twice the age of his oldest son, who is himself twice the age of the middle son, who is twice the age of the youngest son. Quite the unique occurrence."

"Ah," I managed. "Yes. Congratulations are in order."

She beamed at me.

Once she'd gone, Holmes turned to me. "Further congratulations will be in order if you can tell me precisely how old Jack is today."

Can you find the answer?

SOLUTION ON PAGE 130

ROCK PAPER SCISSORS

Wiggins grinned at me. "You've not played Rock Paper Scissors before, Doctor?"

"Doesn't ring a bell," I told him.

"Two of you randomly pick one of the three, and shout your choice simultaneously. There are hand gestures, too. If you both get the same, it's a draw. Otherwise, scissors beats paper, paper beats rock, and rock beats scissors."

"So it's a way of settling an argument," I suggested.

"You were brought up wrong, Doctor," Wiggins said gravely. "Look, try it this way. I played a series of ten games with Alice earlier. I picked scissors six times, rock three times, and paper once. She picked scissors four times, rock twice, and paper four times. None of our games were drawn." He glanced at Holmes, who nodded. "So then, Doctor. What was the overall score for the series?"

SOLUTION ON PAGE 130

ART

One of my medical patients came to see me with a sore arm, but he seemed far more interested in his financial situation than his medical one. It can be that way for some people, particularly men in my experience – aversion to considering unpleasant medical possibilities leads them to emphatic fixation on something utterly unrelated. The fellow just had a light sprain, but that didn't stop him rabbiting on about some art dealing he'd been attempting.

Despite my best attempts otherwise, he resolutely insisted on informing me that he'd sold two paintings the day before, each for £75. One of these produced a 25 per cent profit, but the other yielded a 25 per cent loss.

I informed him absent-mindedly that it could have been worse.

"Not at all," he replied. "It was a very bad day."

I back-pedalled a little to avoid offence, and told him I was referring to his arm. But do you know what he was talking about?

SOLUTION ON PAGE **131**

DAISY

Mrs Hudson was collecting teacups from our rooms, and tutting to herself at the various places where the blessed things had ended up. When she hit a round dozen cups, she let out an enormous sigh, and turned to me.

"Have I mentioned my cousin Daisy?" she asked.

"Not that I recall, Mrs Hudson," I said.

"She's had two children so far. One of them is a boy."

I fought to keep my bemusement off my face. "Oh?"

"How probable do you think it is that the other is a girl?"

Across the room, Holmes chuckled.

Can you find the answer?

SOLUTION ON PAGE  131

THE FOURTH WORDKNOT

I'd barely blurted the answer to Holmes' devilish two-fours puzzle when he produced a slip of paper with a flourish and a quite evil smirk, and handed that over too. Sure enough, it proved to be one of his wordknots, and a stern one to boot. I looked wistfully out of the window, at the rather fine afternoon I was missing, and set myself back to work.

The paper bore the letters:

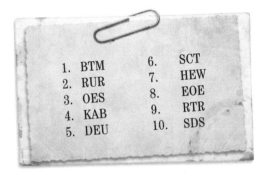

1. BTM
2. RUR
3. OES
4. KAB
5. DEU
6. SCT
7. HEW
8. EOE
9. RTR
10. SDS

Each row held one letter from each of three words, jumbled into no particular order. These letters were all from the same position in each word, and presented in correct sequence, so that the first row held the first letters, the second row held the second letters, and so on and so forth. My task, of course, was to discover what the three ten-letter words were. I knew only that they would be loosely related.

SOLUTION ON PAGE  132

THE ENTHUSIAST

Colin White's murder came as a nasty shock to the London chess-playing community, particularly when police let it be known that they suspected that a fellow player, Brian Campbell, was one of three men who'd visited White that last day, according to a diary entry from that morning. A fellow player of some repute, he'd often been quite critical of White's eccentricities. In addition to Campbell, another chess-player had paid White a visit, a younger man named Tom Wilton, who was said to rather look up to the deceased. Finally, he'd also had a visit from his cousin, Alan Lloyd, a genial chap with a devout love of fishing. Unfortunately, White had listed the men in alphabetical order, rather than time.

Inspector Lestrade was somewhat beside himself, because, following legal advice, none of the men were prepared to make any sort of statement whatsoever. Holmes agreed to help, and a few hours later, he and I were in the dead man's flat.

"We've kept it as it was," Lestrade told us. "We found him in the sitting room, stabbed."

The room was large and restrained. The big central table held four chess boards, one of them set up with a match in the mid-game. I am no chess expert, but I could tell white was winning handily, dominating the board with a line of major pieces, its bishops immediately either side of a rook. Aside from that, there were some small pieces of Greek statuary, a long shelf of books – on chess, inevitably – and a plain ashtray. I considered that perhaps a game had gone badly astray.

Holmes poked around, examined a couple of books, and then turned to Lestrade. "The identity of the murderer is blindingly obvious," he said.

I didn't know what he meant at the time. Do you?

SOLUTION ON PAGE **132**

THE SEVEN

Mrs Hudson eyed me grudgingly from over her stack of retrieved teacups. "My cousin Daisy took her two and her sister Allie's five to see a Punch and Judy show last week," she said.

"Oh, yes, the Neapolitan puppet thing," I replied. Visions of devils, mistresses, and wanton violence floated before my mind's eye. "Is that entirely suitable for children?"

"It is nowadays," she said. "More or less. They apparently enjoyed it anyway, the scamps. But that's not the point. The point is that there are three girls amongst the seven, and four boys, and they sat themselves utterly haphazardly in a row. What do you think that the chance was that the end-spots were both occupied by girls?"

That stopped me in my tracks. Can you work it out?

SOLUTION ON PAGE  133

BRIDGE

The game of bridge is an interesting new Russian spin on that perennial pub favourite, whist. One of the things about it which I find the most curious is its seemingly boundless propensity to end up in the newspapers. It seems nowadays that hardly a week goes by without some mention of it in either the *The Times* or the *Evening Standard*.

The other day, I came across a story about a quartet of bridge players each of whom had been dealt all 13 cards of one suit – a phenomenon known as the "perfect deal".

Dismissing those perfect deals that arise from deliberate tampering or ineffective shuffling, how many such events would you expect to occur nationally over the course of one year?

SOLUTION ON PAGE (133)

THE SECOND CAMOUFLAGE

After an unpleasantly long chase through the eastern portion of the City of London, Holmes and I had successfully apprehended a fellow by the name of Raphael Stevens. He was up to his neck in *The Adventure of the Sapphire Gin*, and there were certain pieces of information which we needed from him. Clearly, he had not been willing to speak to us. I was forced to restrain him while Holmes put his questions.

Eventually, we had the knowledge we needed. I let Stevens go, and slumped against a wall, exhausted – which, naturally, was the exact moment when Holmes decided to challenge me with one of his word camouflages.

"Displayable," he said. "Hideosities. Totipotent. Browbeaten."

A groan escaped me. "Really, Holmes?" I asked.

"Crime never waits for your convenience," he said, severely.

So I had to find the answer. Four shorter words, one per longer word, that formed a thematically linked set.

Can you find the theme?

SOLUTION ON PAGE 134

THE RIBBONS

This particular puzzle was another of Holmes' abstract contrivances, inspired, so far as I was ever aware, by a conversation that he had with Mrs Hudson.

The situation is as follows. Four mother-and-daughter pairs went to purchase ribbon, and over the course of the afternoon, two coincidences could be noted. One was that each mother bought twice as many yards of ribbon as her daughter; the other that each purchaser acquired exactly as many yards of ribbon as the cost of that ribbon per yard in pennies. As examples of that last fact, consider that someone buying one-penny-a-yard ribbon would have purchased one yard, or that someone buying two pence ribbon would have purchased two yards.

In addition to these two foundational coincidences, there are some other pieces of information. Rose purchased two yards more than Daisy. Lily purchased three yards less than Mrs Brown. Mrs White spent 76 pence more than Mrs Black. Daisy spent 48 pence less than Mrs Green.

If Daisy purchased ribbon at four pence a yard, what is Heather's mother named?

SOLUTION ON PAGE  134

BILLY AND JONNY

O ne Easter Saturday, Mrs Hudson fell to discussing the family members she was expecting to see on the following day. Apparently, it was quite the gathering of the clan, because her recitation lasted a while. Unfortunately, she must have noticed that my attention was flagging, along with my good humour, my vital energies, and my will to live.

———◆◆◆———

"Have I mentioned my cousin Trish?" Mrs Hudson asked, after a brief pause.

"Possibly," I said, startled into frankness.

"She has a pair of sons, you know. Billy and Jonny. Apparently, 18 more than the total of their ages added together comes out at twice Billy's age, whilst six less than the difference between their ages comes out at Jonny's age. What age would that make them?"

Can you find the answer?

SOLUTION ON PAGE  135

TROUT

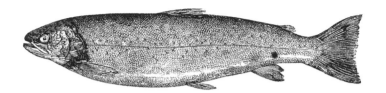

"There's going to be a number of things on the table for lunch tomorrow," Mrs Hudson told me. "It being Easter and all. My cousin Richard managed to get hold of a lovely trout this morning, so that's going to be poached in a light cream and wine sauce, with chives. There'll be new potatoes to go with it, I'd imagine."

"Sounds very pleasant," I ventured.

"I'm sure it will be," she said. "I asked Richard how big the thing was. You know how fishermen love to boast. Well, he only went and told me that the head weighed the same as the combined weight of the tail and half the body, that the body weighed as much as the head and tail together, and that the tail came out at nine ounces. I'm sure you can see what that means."

I kept my own counsel on the implications of that statement, and nodded.

How much does the fish weigh?

SOLUTION ON PAGE 135

GETTING TO MARKET

During our hunt for C. L. Nolan in the course of *The Adventure of the Wandering Bishops*, Holmes and I had to get from Hook, the much-decayed ancient capital town of Hookland, to Coreham, the current capital. In Hookland, they say that Coreham is a cursed city, and there were moments when I felt rather sympathetic to such superstitious claims.

To our moderate annoyance, the only vehicle available to transport us from Hook to Coreham was a mouldering trap pulled by an equally mouldering old nag. The driver was little better than his conveyance, and showed a remarkable lack of anything resembling sense. Had it not been for a heavy case that Holmes was carrying, we could just have walked. It would have been faster and less aggravating.

After 20 frustratingly slow minutes in the trap, I asked the fellow how far we'd come from Hook.

"Halfways as far as to Doglick from here," mumbled the driver.

I got him to repeat the name, just to be sure I'd heard him correctly. Doglick turned out to be a flyspeck of a hamlet every bit as unprepossessing as its name. Some five miles after we'd got clear of the place, I made the mistake of again asking the driver as to our progress, specifically, how much further it was to Coreham.

His answer, word for word, was identical.

I asked no further questions, and an hour later, we finally arrived in Coreham, which is at least a pretty place.

Can you tell how far it is from Hook to Coreham?

SOLUTION ON PAGE 136

THE FIFTH WORDKNOT

Holmes handed me my fifth and final wordknot one quiet afternoon when I was well rested and refreshed, and more than a little bored. I peered at both him and the slip of paper cautiously, half-expecting lions to leap from behind a cupboard the moment I took it from him, or some such terrifying crisis.

As it was, nothing more distressing happened than Holmes smiling at me, which of course unsettled me colossally. The slip of paper bore the following:

1. BAH
2. BAI
3. LOA
4. CCO
5. PET
6. HEN
7. ROY
8. TIS
9. AEI
10. SSL

The task was to unscramble the letters to find three loosely-themed ten-letter words, working from the basis that the first line of the text comprised their initial letters, the second line their second letters, and so on.

It was not easy.

Can you do it?

SOLUTION ON PAGE 137

PENCILS

During *The Adventure of the Third Carriage*, Holmes had the need to spend a day masquerading as a wholesaler of stationery. He returned from this outing much vexed, so naturally I asked him whether his investigations had gone well.

"Oh, yes, very useful," he said. "I got the information I was after."

"But something appears to be bothering you nonetheless," I replied.

He sighed. "The stationery business is cripplingly ineffective. It irks me to have had to pretend to approve of such ridiculous business practices."

"I see," I said. This was not strictly a true or accurate statement.

"Imagine this," Holmes said. "A box of 160 pencils, in eight rows of 20."

"Sounds about right."

"No!" Holmes sighed again. "You could get ten per cent more pencils to a box in a heartbeat."

Can you see how?

SOLUTION ON PAGE 137

TWO WRONGS

Holmes called me in to his laboratory area one morning. When I got there, curious as to what oddity I might be shown, I discovered that he'd written a very curious equation on the blackboard: WRONG + WRONG = RIGHT.

"You appear to be flying in the face of modern ethics, my dear friend," I told him.

"Appearances can be deceptive," he replied. "This, for example, is a perfectly regular mathematical addition, except that eight of the ten digits from zero to nine have been replaced, in no particular order, with the eight letters that make up the words 'wrong' and 'right'."

"Ingenious," I said.

"Glad you think so, old chap. See if you can find a solution."

Can you do it?

SOLUTION ON PAGE (138)

EASTER SPIRIT

Holmes gestured grandly towards the coffee table. "There are four eggs," he began.

"I hate to disagree, old chap," I said. "There don't appear to be any eggs there at all."

He smirked at me. "Where's your Easter spirit?"

"Not on the coffee table, that's for sure."

"There are four eggs, Watson. If they are not physically present, they are certainly there metaphorically."

"I dare say I can accept that," I said.

"One of the four is three inches in length. The other three are smaller, and all I will tell you of them is that they collectively equal the volume of the larger egg, that they are all precisely similar in shape to their larger cousin, and that they differ from each other in length by half an inch from short to medium, and by half an inch from medium to long."

I sighed. "I suppose you want me to puzzle out their lengths?"

"Just that of the shortest of all will do."

Can you find the answer?

SOLUTION ON PAGE

138

THREE MEN

"**I** came across an interesting little exercise that might benefit you, Watson. It'll test your powers of reasoning, and nothing else."

I put down my book, and grabbed a pencil and notepad. "Fire away, old chap."

"Excellent. On a theoretical train, the conductor, driver and ticket inspector are, in no particular order, named Smith, Jones and Robinson. As luck – or, in this instance, contrivance – would have it, there are also three passengers with the same surnames, whom I will refer to as Mr Smith, Mr Jones, and Mr Robinson, in order to distinguish them from that train's staff."

"Very well," I said.

"There are several pieces of information I can give you. One, Mr Robinson lives in Brixton, whilst the conductor lives in Chelsea. Two, Mr Jones cannot do algebra. Three, Smith regularly beats the ticket inspector at billiards. Four, the passenger who shares the conductor's name lives in Tottenham. Finally, five, the conductor shares his local pub with the passenger who works as a professor of mathematical physics at University College, London."

I frantically finished jotting down notes. "I have all that," I told Holmes.

"In that case, please be so good as to let me know the name of the driver. I'll warn you now that there is insufficient information to calculate every particular of every man, but there is enough to identify the driver."

Can you find the solution?

SOLUTION ON PAGE **139**

RUFUS

When Holmes and I met with Wiggins one afternoon, he was accompanied by a rather scrappy-looking mutt, who eyed me with evident suspicion.

"This is Rufus," Wiggins said. "He's a friend."

"Charmed," I said.

"He's very energetic," Wiggins told us. "Just this morning, he and I set out for a little walk."

At the word 'walk', the dog barked happily.

"When we set out, he immediately dashed off to the end of the road, then turned round and bounded back to me. He did this four times in total, in fact. After that, he settled down to match my speed, and we walked the remaining 81 feet to the end of the road at my pace. But it seems to me that if I tell you the distance from where we started to the end of the road, which is 625 feet, and that I was walking at four miles an hour, you ought to be able to work out how fast Rufus goes when he's running."

"Indeed we should," said Holmes, and turned to look at me expectantly.

What's the dog's running speed?

SOLUTION ON PAGE  140

MANUAL

I was at the table, reading my paper, when Holmes appeared from his study. "I have a little something for you, Watson," he said. "It might prove more educational than the cricket scores."

"I suppose anything is possible," I said, and moved my paper.

In its place, Holmes set down three truncated cones made of paper, and ten pennies. I eyed them uncertainly.

"Do you think it possible to distribute those pennies between these makeshift paper cups so that each cup contains an odd number of pennies, with no pennies left over?"

I thought about it for a moment. "No."

He clapped me on the shoulder. "Let me know when you've succeeded."

Can you see the solution?

SOLUTION ON PAGE **140**

THE TYRANT

"**I** should warn you, Watson, that I am a vengeful, bloody-minded tyrant."

I looked round at Holmes, and deliberately kept my face straight. "I've long suspected it," I told him.

"Which is why I'm about to have you executed," he replied. "Luckily for you, my religion permits you a get-out clause."

"That's a relief," I said.

"I will present you with two identical large jars, along with 50 white marbles, and 50 black marbles. You are to distribute these marbles between the two jars however you wish, so long as all 100 are used. One of these jars will then be chosen at random, and if you withdraw a white marble from it, your life will be spared."

"That seems oddly specific for a religion."

"It's an oddly specific religion," Holmes replied. "How would you maximize your chances of escape?"

SOLUTION ON PAGE

TERMINUS

Maxwell Perry had died in a small alley just the right side of Brick Lane, shot in the chest. His attire suggested that he'd been in something of a panic – his shoes were unlaced, his trousers belted but unbuttoned, and his jumper both back to front and inside out. Profound though his alarm had clearly been, it had just as clearly not saved him.

As investigations unfolded, it became clear that Perry was involved in the opium trade, moving his death towards natural causes. Unfortunately, he was also a distant cousin of someone of note, and poor Inspector Lestrade was on the receiving end of a considerable amount of pressure to solve the murder. Having a whole pile of witnesses and suspects didn't help.

Holmes grudgingly agreed to have a look over Lestrade's notes, mainly to get the fellow out of our rooms. When they arrived he flicked through them, making desultory comments as he went. "Brinton claims to have seen the victim running past like 'a sack of monkeys', whatever that means... Murphy heard a shot, and found the body, but didn't see anyone else, which seems short-sighted at best... Bligh remembers seeing the victim running away because of the visible jumper label... Colgate saw one man shoot another, face-to-face, but was too far to get even the slightest useful detail... Routledge found a pistol in a waste skip behind a pub... Oliver says the victim turned a corner and almost barrelled into him, then shrieked and dashed off..." He dropped the file. "That's more than enough, I think. It's quite blatant who killed the man."

What did Holmes mean?

SOLUTION ON PAGE 142

THE FINAL CAMOUFLAGE

In sharp contrast to the gentle circumstances in which Holmes assigned me his final wordknot, he waited until I was actively ill with a heavy cold before tasking me with his final camouflage. I was feeling thoroughly sorry for myself that morning, not to mention fuzzy-headed, and I did not respond particularly well. Holmes, of course, was utterly unbothered, so in the end I worked on his puzzle anyway.

The four words that he assigned me were gatecrashed, hyperboles, subceiling and godfathered. My task was to find the small words hidden with the larger, one per word, such that the four small words were grouped together by a loose theme.

Can you discover the theme?

SOLUTION ON PAGE 142

SEVEN APPLEWOMEN

A rather odd affair, this one. It was inspired, once again, by Hookland. Holmes said that he came across it in an old book, and felt that it would serve as an unusually stringent test of my poor, battered faculties. Like many of its ilk, it is contrived to the point of utter lunacy, but even so, it may prove interesting.

In a Hookland market, there are seven applewomen, who have the suspiciously regularized amounts of 20, 40, 60, 80, 100, 120, and 140 apples to sell. Being friends – and somewhat peculiar – they decide on a variable pricing scheme for their wares which will ensure that when each sells her entire consignment, each will come away with the same amount of money. Why they didn't just pool up all the takings and divide them equally is quite beyond me. Perhaps it's due to the same religious requirements that forced Holmes' theoretical tyranny to give the condemned a basket of marbles.

Still... Can you work out the pricing scheme?

SOLUTION ON PAGE **143**

FIENDISH

ANSWERS AND SOLUTIONS

"The bigger the crime the more obvious, as a rule, is the motive."

Sherlock Holmes

THE WEIGHTS

30lb. The three together weight 180lb, and man and child are 162lb more than the dog, so the dog weighs half the difference between 162 and 180. 180 − 162 = 18/2 = 9. The dog is 30 per cent of the child's weight. 9/30*100 = 30, giving us the weight of the baby.

SOLARIS

Since the Sun appears to rise in the east, the Earth revolves counterclockwise on its axis. So at true midnight by local time, the Earth is spinning you in exactly the same direction as it is moving around the Sun, and at true midday, it is spinning you in exactly the opposite direction. Therefore you are going faster at midnight. At a point near the equator (less as you move towards the poles), your speed varies by about 0.3 miles per second either way from Earth's base speed of around 18 miles per second around the Sun. But don't worry, the Sun itself (with our solar system, obviously) is moving at up to 500 miles per second through the universe, so your variation in speed is quite minor.

A WORSHIP OF WRITERS

Tomkins. From the information given, Squires must be the playwright, Appleby the historian, Whitely the humorist, Archer the poet, Gardner the short-story writer, and Tomkins the novelist.

LOGGERS

360 cubic feet of wood, which works out at a little over 2.8 cords. The relative amount of time Doug and Dave spend sawing and splitting must match the ratio of how much of each job they can perform in one day – that is, they must divide their day by 6:9, or 2:3. Thus they must spend 3/5ths of the day sawing, which is slower, and 2/5ths of the day splitting. 3/5ths of 600 is 360 cubic feet of wood (as is 2/5ths of 900).

THE FIRST WORDKNOT

The words were violinists, trumpeters and pianoforte.

TWO SUMS

This question has a few possible answers: $12 + 93 = 48 + 57$ ($=$ 105), $13 + 74 = 28 + 59$ ($= 87$), or $173 + 4 = 85 + 92$ ($= 177$). Bearing in mind that larger and smaller numbers will average towards median numbers will help this discovery, and if there is a way to find the answers without trial and error, I do not know it.

DUCK DUCK GOOSE

Four shillings. Starting with 1 for a chicken gives you 2 for a duck, which, in the second equation of $3c + d = 2g$ would mean that $3*1 + 1*2 = 2*goose = 5$. But we can't have 2.5 shillings for a goose. So double the chicken and duck prices. $3*2 + 1*4 = 10$, giving 5 for a goose. Try that in the third equation of $3g + 1c + 2d = 25$. $3*5 + 1*2 + 2*4 = 15 + 2 + 8 = 25$. So 5s, 4s and 2s are the correct prices, and a duck is 4s.

THE JEWELLER

75 minutes. If going to and from work by cab takes 30 minutes, one way takes 15 minutes. The walking part of the journey with a return cab must be 15 minutes less than the combined time. 90 − 15 = 75 minutes.

THE NOTE

13 21 13 21 32 21 12. Speak the digits aloud, and it will become clear that each line is described by the numbers in the following line – so "One 2"; then "One one, one two"; then "Three 1s, one 2," and so on.

SERPENTINE

The level of the water will fall slightly. If Sieger sinks, he must be denser than water on average. When an item floats, it displaces water equal to its weight, but when submerged, displaces water equal to its volume. Since he sinks, he's heavier than the amount of water his volume would weigh, and suddenly takes up less displaced water, lowering the water level.

THE LEGACY

£24. We know that x + y = 100, and that x/4 − y/3 = 11. Multiply out the divisors in that second equation (i.e. *12), and you get 3x − 4y = 132. Now x = 100 − y, so 3*(100 − y) − 4y = 132, and 300 − 3y − 4y = 132, or 7y = 300 − 132 = 168. So, y = 168/7 = 24. (And x, Frederick's bequest, must be £76).

CHILDREN

Three of one and one of the other is more likely. There are 16 possibilities (two options, four times = $2^4 = 16$), all equally likely. Of those, two are single-gender, BBBB and GGGG. Eight are 3–and–1: BGGG, GBGG, GGBG, GGGB, and their opposites. Six are two of each – BBGG, BGBG, BGGB, and their opposites. So there's a 8/16 (or 50 per cent) chance of three children of one gender, a 6/16 (or 37.5 per cent) chance of two of each gender, and a 2/16 (or 12.5 per cent) chance of all the children being the same gender. As an aside, do note that about one human pregnancy in 90 produces twins, which may somewhat complicate a more precise calculation, and in practice, the chance of a male birth is very rarely exactly 50 per cent, so the terms of this question are not rigorous reflections of reality.

THE REVENGE

Blaydon refers to the *Revenge* as "it", not "she", in direct contravention of all English-speaking naval tradition.

THE TRUNK

35 yards. We don't know the tractor's speed, but it moves a certain distance – Y – for each pace Holmes takes. So when he has moved 140 yards, the front of the tree has moved 140Y yards. Holmes has walked that distance plus the length of the tree, x, in that time, so in yards, $140 = x + 140Y$. In the other direction, Holmes has walked 20 paces, so the tip of the tree has moved 20Y yards. Since they're going in opposite directions, their combined distance equals the length of the tree, and $x = 20 + 20Y$. So now we have $x = 20 + 20Y$, and $x = 140 – 140Y$. So $20 + 20Y = 140 – 140Y$, and $1 + Y = 7 – 7Y$, thus $8Y = 6$, or $Y = 0.75$. Since $x = 20 + 20Y$, then $x = 20 + 15 = 35$ yards.

THE FIELD

40 days. Let us measure in a unit of "fields per day", so we then have $C + G = 1/45$, $C + L = 1/60$, and $G + L = 1/90$. Our first task is to compare like with like. The lowest common denominator of those fractions is $1/360$th. So $1C + 1G + 0L = 8/360$, $1C + 0G + 1L = 6/360$, and $0C + 1G + 1L = 4/360$. Substituting the first equation (ordered to solve for C) $C = (8/360 - 1G)$, into the second, so $(8/360 - 1G) + 1L = 6/360$, and $2/360 + 1L = 1G$. Substitute this into the third, $2/360 + 1L + 1L = 4/360$, or $L = 1/360$. Track back to the second now to solve for G, and $2 + 360 + 1/360 = G = 3/360$, and finally back once more for $C = 8/360 - 3/360 = 5/360$. So the lamb eats $1/360$th of a field a day, the goat $3/360$ths, and the cow $5/360$ths. Since they're all in there together, they get through $1+3+5=9/360$ths of a field a day. $360/9 = 40$, so they'll eat all the grass in 40 days.

THE TYPE

27. In order to be able to form each month in full, you need the following 27 letters – AA, B, C, D, EEE, F, G, H, I, J, L, M, N, OO, P, RR, S, T, UU, V, and Y.

THE STABBING

The butler. He claims to have tripped over the body in the darkness, and yet to have seen the victim lying on the floor from outside the room. He's clearly lying.

THE MANAGER

36. Go back x years, and the deputy was half the manager's current age, making him 24, and the manager the deputy's current age, y. So $y - x = 24$, and because the difference between ages will stay constant, $y + x = 48$. Thus $2y = 72$, and the deputy is 36.

BALANCE

No matter how a coin is weighted, if you flip it twice, it will always generate a head immediately followed by a tails precisely as often as it generates a tails immediately followed by a head. So throw the coin twice. Then HT is one fair possibility, and TH is the other. If you get any other result, throw the coin twice more. On the most blatantly weighted coins, you might require some patience, but the toss will remain fair. Obviously you'll be waiting a very, very long time if the coin has two identical faces.

GETTING AHEAD

It took me a while, and a little prompting, but eventually I hit on volumetric comparison by submersion in water. For example, you could fill a bucket with water, and place it inside an empty tub. Submerge the waxed head in the bucket, and water equal to its volume will spill into the tub. Pour this run-off into one of several similar glass jars. You can then re-fill the bucket, and submerge the vegetable into the bucket, again gathering the over-spill. Compare the run-offs, and you'll be able to see which is closest to the original. I have never come across this story in any other source, so for now, please consider it whimsy rather than historical truth.

BICYCLE

The trick is to divide our journey by the ratio of our comparative speeds – 5:4, in this instance. So as the faster walker and slower rider, Holmes would ride for 4/9ths of the way, and I, in the opposite situation, would ride 5/9ths of the way. If we each do our riding in one stint, it doesn't make any difference who goes first. Either Holmes could ride eight miles, then leave the bicycle for me to pick up, and walk; or I could ride ten miles, leaving the bicycle for Holmes to pick up. The trip will take three hours, with each of us riding for one hour and walking for two, and the bicycle waiting for an hour in the middle.

THE CANVAS

10" x 20". Normally, in finding a maximum density for a rectilinear object, one would get as close to a square as possible. But having the top and bottom margins be twice those of the left and right requires that the piece be twice as tall as it is wide in order to minimize dead space. So the canvas needs to be 20" tall and 10" wide, and the picture 12" tall and 6" high.

PIG

15. Either you found this easy, or you need to hold on to your hats, my friends. It is genuinely straightforward, but it requires several steps. We know that $95x + 97y = 4,238$, and that the numbers of both pigs and sheep must be non-zero integers. Indeterminate equation theory allows a solution. First, solve our equation for x, where $x = (4238/95) - (97y/95)$, and reduce the right-hand side into integers and fractions as far as possible: $x = 44 + 58/95 - y - 2y/95$, which simplifies to $x = 44 - y + (58-2y)/95$. Now, since x is an integer, the right-hand term also must be an integer. As 44 and y are both integers as well, that last bit $(58-2y)/95$ must also be an integer, albeit one we are utterly unsure of. Let's call that value "2i" just for now. We can then rearrange our new definition of $2i = (58-2y)/95$ in terms of y as $y = 29 - 95i$. But y is an non-negative integer, so $0 <= 29 - 95i$, and $i <= 29/95$. We now have a term for y that we can substitute back in the equation for x, so $x = 44 - (29 - 95i) + (58 - 2*(29 - 95i))95$, and although that looks ugly, a lot of it cancels out, and it simplifies down to $x = 44 - 29 + 95i + 2i$, or $x = 15 + 97i$. Again, x must be an integer, so $0 <= 15 + 97i$, and $-15/97 <= i$. So now we have a range where $-15/97 <= i <= 29/95$, and since i also has to be an integer, in this case it must be 0. Finally, we have equations for both x and y expressed in terms of i, so $x = 15 + 97*0$, or 15, and $y = 29 - 95*0$, or 29. Pigs were x, so he bought 15 pigs. You can approach any indeterminate equation using this method, although equations with more unknowns require commensurately more steps.

If the equation is insoluble, your range for i will be impossible.

THE SECOND WORDKNOT

The three words were *picaresque*, *dishonesty* and *mountebank*, and the theme was roguery.

THE SHOPKEEPER

Digits to make up a larger number. In this instance, they were brass, and clearly intended to screw into a front door to display the house number.

MATCH TWO

Take ten matches, and use them to spell out the word FIVE. Then remove seven of the ten matches, leaving just the letters IV, "4" in Roman numerals. Simple when you know how – but then, most puzzles are.

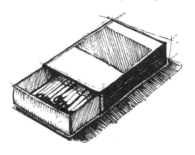

CURIO

3&5, and 7&8. To solve this mathematically, we need to address a little more indeterminacy. We know that $x^2 + x*y + y^2 = a$ square number. We can use $(x - a*y)^2$ to represent the square number, as this will always be squared, and the variable term "a" allows us to come to any square for a given x,y. We can then expand this square term from $(x - ay)*(x - ay)$ to $x^2 - 2axy + (a^2)(y^2)$. From that, we can see that $x + y = ya^2 - 2ax$. Add $(-y + 2ax)$ to each side again, and it will simplify down to $x + 2ax = ya^2 - y$, and $x(2a + 1) = y(a^2 - 1)$. Therefore, as the terms have to balance out to $xy = yx$, then $x = a^2 - 1$, and $y = 2a + 1$. When $a = 1$, this gives us 0,2 for x,y – which works, but we need numbers from 1–9. So $a = 2$ gives 3,5, and $a = 3$ gives 8,7. Note that $a = 4$ gives x>9. Personally, I stuck to the brute force solution.

SIX FEET UNDER

Ten feet below the surface, the seasonal temperatures in the temperate zone are up to four months behind air temperature. If it was the end of spring on the surface, it would still have been winter for the moles and earthworms. Below 75 feet or so, there is almost no seasonal variation at all – at least, here in London.

ENGINE TROUBLE

200 miles. Say x is the distance from the spot where the engine fault developed to the destination, and y is full speed. We then know that the normal time "t" to complete the journey is $t = x/y$, that at 3/5ths of y, the time is $t + 2 = 5x/3y$, and that if we'd gone 50 miles further we'd have arrived 1 hour 20 minutes late, so $t + 4/3 = 50/y + 5(x – 50)/3y$. Substitute $t = x/y$ through the second equation, and you'll quickly find that t has to be 3, and $x = 3y$. So we would normally have had three hours left to go, making a typical four-hour journey, and the distance left would have had to be three times the normal top speed in miles per hour. Now we know the third equation gets us there 2/3 of an hour sooner than the second, so substitute $t + 2 = 5x/3y$ into the third equation, and $5x/3y – 2/3 = 50/y + 5x/3y – 250/3y$, so $5x – 2y = 150 + 5x – 50$, and $2y = 100$. Thus full speed is 50mph and, finally, our full distance takes four hours at 50mph to travel, so must be 200 miles.

RECALL

28. Start at the back and work forwards, reversing the operations as you go, and it is easy. $2*10 = 20$, $-8 = 12$, $*12 = 144$, $+ 52 = 196$, sq rt $= 14$, $* 3/2 = 21$, $* 7 = 147$, $* 4/7 = 84$, $/ 3 = 28$. Note that $*4/7$ reverses $+ 75$ per cent because $4/4 + 3/4 = 7/4$.

MORAN

Yes, actually. You need to remember that the first shot marks the start of the time count, and so counts as $t = 0$, not $t = 5s$. To meet his boast precisely, the gun would have had to shoot 60 rounds in 4 minutes and 55 seconds. The same principle is why if you put two points on a piece of paper, one line segment connects them rather than two.

THE MURDER OF MOLLY GLASS

Mrs Glass had lit the fire in her bedroom before going to sleep. Once she was slumbering, her husband turned off the gas line to the house. The fire duly went out. Then he switched the gas back on again, so that it built up unhindered in her bedroom, and asphyxiated her.

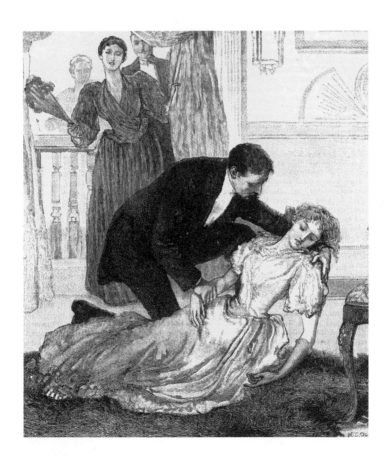

THE THIRD WORDKNOT

The words are *hoodwinked, handcuffed* and *restrained*.

BARNABAS

Two half-crowns. We know the work-rate of both people is consistent between the two tasks. Wiggins can shovel as quickly as Barnabas can dig, but he can dig four times faster than Barnabas can shovel. There are two steps required in comparing Wiggins digging to Barnabas digging, but as the work-rate is the same in both steps, Wiggins' work rate is two to Barnabas' one. So however they broke down the jobs, and however long it took, Wiggins was twice as good a worker as Barnabas, and the money should be split 2:1.

CUNNING

ANSWERS AND SOLUTIONS

"There is nothing more deceptive than an obvious fact."

Sherlock Holmes

THE FORTY-FOUR

20 and 64. You could use trial and error to find two plausible ages 44 years apart that multiply to 1280, but there is also an algebraic solution. We have $x*y = 1280$ and $x - y = 44$. So $x = 44 + y$. This gives us $44y + y^2 = 1280$, or reordering into a standard quadratic, $y^2 + 44y - 1280 = 0$. From the quadratic formula, $y = (-b +- \text{sq root } (b^2 - 4ac))/2a$, where a, b and c are the multiples of each term in order. Note that +– means you have to solve twice, once adding the square root, and once subtracting it. In our case, a is 1 (for just y^2), b is 44, and $c = -1280$. So we have $(-44 +- \text{sq rt } (44^2 - (4*1* - 1280))) / 2$, which once you sort out the arithmetic, breaks down to $(-44 +- 84) / 2 = -64$ and $+20$. We're just looking for magnitudes for the ages (the single minus arrives since we were given the difference between the two ages, not the sum), so Michael is 64 and Minnie is 20.

PIPE DREAMS

Definitely not in one generation, no. Roughly half of pregnancies produce boys, so initially, half of the mothers would stop producing children. Of those that remained, again roughly half would produce boys, and stop. This pattern would continue indefinitely. At each stage, the expectant mothers remaining would produce as many boys as girls, so the gender balance would not change, but the number of children would plummet, and the population contract.

It is not impossible that some women might have a genetic predisposition to produce more girls than boys, and this genetic trait would become highly selected for, but it takes an average of 75 generations or more for a mutation to spread through the population. Even a strongly selected pressure like this would still require hundreds of years to have a noticeable effect.

THE OLD ONES

The murderer was in the process of robbing the pub, and shot the victim to eliminate him as a witness. In fact, he had already murdered the landlord and the cook, at which point one more body would hardly matter. The fellow was eventually apprehended at Portsmouth Docks, and duly hung.

RIFLE ROUNDS

Ninety-seven. Between boxes of 15 and 20, you can make any multiple of five, so long as that is not five, ten, or 25. So the general technique to solve any request is, if the number is not already a multiple of five, provide boxes of 18 until you are left with a multiple of five, and then assemble the remainder from the other boxes. The last time when this technique falls down is the number 97, where subsequent boxes of 18 leave 79, 61, 43, and finally 25. Once you get any higher, up to five boxes of 18 will always be enough to bring you to a multiple of five that you can fill. Quite ingenious.

THE PLEASANT WAY

18 miles. As a general rule for this sort of problem, triple the distance of the first meeting place, and subtract the distance of the second meeting place. So 10*3 − 12 = 18.

FASHION

Twenty dresses. If there are x dresses costing y each, then x*y = 1800. Furthermore, we also know that (x + 30)*(y − 3) = 1800. Since y = 1800/x, then (x + 30)*(1800/x − 3) = 1800, and 1800/(x + 30) + 3 = 1800/x. Thus 3*(x + 30)x + 1800x = 1800(x + 30), and $3x^2 + 90x − 54000 = 0$. We've discussed solving quadratic equations earlier; the solution to this gives you a positive quadratic root of x = 120. There were 120 dresses, each costing an eye-watering £15, of which 20 had been stolen.

THE FIRST CAMOUFLAGE

The words are *cut*, *dig*, *sow* and *trim*, and their unifying theme is gardening (or, more generally, agriculture, I suppose).

THE APPLE MARKET

The truth is that the two sales methods are only directly equivalent when the number of apples sold at three a penny is in the proportion of 3:2 with the apples sold at two a penny. However, that is not the case here; the proportion is 1:1. If the first woman had had 36 apples, and the second 24, then they would have been due 12 pence each, whether they'd sold them themselves or via the friend. In this case, the three-a-penny lady would have earned 10 pence from her apples, and her friend 15 pence, so by splitting the money into two lots of 12 pence, the first woman gets 2 pence extra, and the second woman 3 pence less. 9.5 pence and 14.5 pence would have been a fairer division.

A PAIR OF FOURS

In the end, it took me a lot of time, not a little. However, I did find the solution – sq rt (sq rt (sq rt 4) ^ 4!). 4! is 1*2*3*4, or 24, and sq rt 4 is obviously 2, so the equation becomes sq rt (sq rt 2)^24, and you can write sq rt as ^0.5. Roots and powers of this sort cancel out, so it becomes $2^0.5^0.5^24 = 2^0.5^12 = 2^6 = 64$.

ASHCOURT STATION

Nine (or possibly 11). As we set off, there were four Waterloo-to-Ashcourt trains en route, one just leaving Waterloo, and one in Ashcourt station. Over the next five hours, four more would depart Waterloo, with a fifth about to depart as we pulled in. Over the course of our journey, we must inevitably pass all of those trains, as there is nowhere else for them to go but past us. Now to my mind, the train in Ashcourt as we departed and the train leaving Waterloo as we arrived don't really count as being "on the way", so I make the tally to be nine. If you decided you did count them, then 11 is a reasonable answer as well.

OLD HOOK

Ten and 5/41sts hours. If Ted rides for x miles at 8 mph, then his journey time = (x/8) + (40 − x)/1. Hob walks for y miles, so his journey time is y/2 + (40 − y)/8. This means that Ern's journey time is x/8 + (x − y)/8 + (40 − y)/8. Now all these total times are equal. So (x/8) + 40 − x = y/2 + (40 − y)/8, which means 7x + 3y = 280. Also, by multiplying the second and third equation by 8, 4y + 40 − y = x + x − y + 40 − y, and 2x − 5y = 0. So now we have two simple equations for x and y. Solve, and we'll find that x = 1400/41, and y = 560/41. Note that leaving it in terms of 1/41 is simplest for this solution. Substitute x into Ted's time or y into Hob's time, and you'll find that the total is ten and 5/41 hours.

ANDREW

Just before leaving for David's house, Andrew would set the clock to 12, and start it. When he arrived at David's, he'd note the correct time from David's clock, and he'd do the same when he left to return home, so he knew how long he'd spent with David. Then when he arrived home, he'd have a record of precisely how long he'd been away in total. Subtracting the time he'd spent at David's from this would tell him how long his journey there and back had been. Adding one half of this amount to the time when he left David's house then gave him the correct time now.

CENTURIAL

53 years and four months. It should be plain that if the youngest son is aged x, then x + 2x + 4x + 8x = 100, so 15x = 100, and x = 6 and 2/3rds years. Jack is 8x years old, so he's 53 and 1/3rd years old (and his sons are 26 and 2/3rds, 13 and 1/3rd, and six and 2/3rds).

ROCK PAPER SCISSORS

Wiggins won, 7–3. Since there were no draws, Wiggins's six scissors met Alice's four paper and 2 rock, giving Wiggins four out of six. The other games must have been Alice's scissors, which met Wiggins' rock three times, and paper once, giving Wiggins three out of four. So he won seven out of ten.

ART

He lost £10 overall. £75 at 25 per cent profit means that painting cost £60 originally. £75 at 25 per cent loss means that the other painting cost £100. So he paid £160 for paintings that fetched £150.

DAISY

The probability is 2/3, or roughly 67 per cent. With two children, there are four possibilities: boy-boy, boy-girl, girl-boy, and girl-girl. We know only that girl-girl is impossible. So there are three options, and in two of them, one of the children is a girl.

THE FOURTH WORDKNOT

The words were *trebuchets, musketeers* and *broadswords.*

THE ENTHUSIAST

The white pieces on the board are in a nearly impossible position. Two bishops of the same colour can never be separated by a single square in a straight line. Well, it is theoretically possible for white to promote a pawn to a second white bishop, I suppose, but such a move would be colossally unlikely, particularly in the mid-game. The board must have been set up by a non-player, and the only person with any motive to stage a scene with a game would be the murderer, so Alan Lloyd was the murderer. When faced with his error, Lloyd confessed.

THE SEVEN

One in seven, or about 14 per cent. It turns out that the total number of ways the children could sit is 5,040, or 7!, which is 7*6*5*4*3*2*1. Since there are three girls, you can assign them into pairs to sit at the ends in six ways. For any given arrangement of two girls at the ends, there are five different ways the children in between could sit, so 5! = 120 options. Six different arrangements of 120 options gives 720 ways there could be a girl at each end. So the chance is 720 in 5,040, or one in seven.

BRIDGE

Absolutely none. The actual chance of a perfect deal occurring in bridge is 2,235,197,406,985,633,368,301,599, 999 to 1. If the entire population of the planet played 60 hands of bridge every day, newborns included, you'd expect one naturally occurring perfect deal to occur slightly more often than once every 125,000,000,000 years. In practice, shuffling a deck of cards is often done ineffectively, and most occurrences of a perfect deal come down to poor randomization. The rest are the result of deliberate tampering.

THE SECOND CAMOUFLAGE

The theme was dining out, and the words
were *lay*, *sit*, *eat* and *tip*.

THE RIBBONS

Mrs White. Remembering that each amount spent must be a
square number, each mother's length of ribbon must be even,
and working through the logic, Daisy bought 4y for 16 pence,
and her mother Mrs Green 8y for 64 pence. Rose bought 6y
for 36 pence, and her mother Mrs Brown bought 12y for 144
pence. Lily bought 9y for 81 pence and her mother Mrs Black
bought 18y for 324 pence. And Heather bought 10y for 100
pence and her mother Mrs White bought 20y for 400 pence.

BILLY AND JONNY

Billy is 30, and Jonny 12. We know $x + y + 18 = 2x$, so $y = x - 18$. We also know that $x - y - 6 = y$, so $2y = x - 6$. Substitute through, and $2x - 30 = x - 6$, so $x = 30$, and thus $y = 12$.

TROUT

72 ounces. If the tail weighs 9, the head must weigh $9 + x/2$, and the body, $x = 18 + x/2$. So half $x = 18$, and $x = 36$, which means the head = 27, and the total is $9 + 27 + 36$.

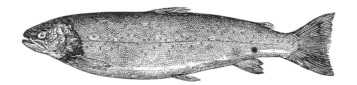

GETTING TO MARKET

Ten miles. After 20 minutes, we had travelled half as far as the distance from that spot to Doglick, so it took an hour to Doglick. Then, five miles past Doglick, we had half that five-mile distance still to go, and that took one hour. So we did five miles in two hours, our total journey time was four hours, and the full distance was ten miles.

THE FIFTH WORDKNOT

The words are *abacterial*, *biocenosis* and *halophytes*,
and their broad theme is biology.

PENCILS

By arranging them in alternating rows of 19 and 20, as it
turns out. By putting the second row in the hollows of the
first, and then the third in the hollows of the second, you save
enough space to get a ninth row in place. So you would have
180 pencils if all the rows were 20 pencils long, but four of
them are one short, giving you 176 – 16 more than 160.

TWO WRONGS

There are 21 separate solutions, but space forbids me from listing them all. 12734 + 12734 = 25468 gives you the smallest sum, and 49306 + 49306 = 98612 the largest, but any of them will do. To solve this, approach the problem with the same sort of logic that was used in the previous puzzle of this sort. For example, R must be either 2W (if R<5) or 2W + 1. The same holds true for I being 2R, 2R + 1, or, if 2R>9, 2R – 10 – where 2R is a maximum of 18, for 2*9. But since I works of 2R, and R works off 2W, I becomes a function of 4W, and since 2I always has to be less than 19, W cannot be more than 4. Besides, if WR was worth more than 49, there would be an extra letter in front of the word "right". Similarly, the O + O = G and G + G = T mean that O also has to be 4 or less. T must always be even, as there is no '1' to carry over from a previous term. The only way the letters W, R, O, N, G can be zero is if the letter before them is worth 5 or more. When you have some limits attached, try assuming a case where, say, O = 0, and you will find that the matter quickly unfolds. Keep attacking in this way, and you will arrive at an effective answer.

EASTER SPIRIT

1.5". Volumes of solids that are the same shape vary according to the cube of their relative lengths. So the largest egg has a comparative volume of 27, being 3" in length. So the volumes of the other three eggs have to add to $27 = x^3 + (x + 0.5)^3 + (x + 1)^3$. *Regula falsi* is probably simpler here than trying to simplify the equation, so try x = 1, for 12.375 (or 2.3^3), and x = 2 for 50.625 (or 3.7^3), and you'll see that 1 and 2 put you the same distance from the correct answer, so the midpoint between 1 and 2 must be where the volumes sum to 3^3. In other words, x = 1.5 inches.

THREE MEN

The driver is called Smith. To find the answer, it is useful to keep a grid of possible (and impossible) associations to help make the facts clearer. From (1), Mr Robinson lives in Brixton and, associating (5), is not the professor. From (2), Mr Jones is not the professor either, so the professor is Mr Smith. From (5), Mr Smith lives near the conductor, so Mr Smith also lives in Chelsea. That means Mr Jones must live in Tottenham, and from (4), the conductor is called Jones. So from (3), the ticket inspector can only be Robinson, which means that the driver is called Smith.

RUFUS

16 mph. The overall distance to the end of the road in feet is 625 = 5^4, and the end of the dog's running time is when the distance in feet is $81 = 3^4$. These quad roots are obviously in the ratio 5:3, so the sum of the two speeds and the difference between the two speeds must be in the ratio of 5:3, and thus the two speeds in the ratio of 4:1. Wiggins walks at 4 mph, so the dog runs at 16 mph.

MANUAL

It is only possible if one cup is inside another, at which point it becomes trivial. So, for example, you could place a penny in one cup, and then two pennies – and the previous cup and its contents – inside a second cup, and then the remaining seven in the third cup. There are many options, but they all boil down to getting the idea that two of the cups must be nested.

THE TYRANT

If I were to split my marbles evenly, 50 in each jar, then the 50/50 chance of getting either jar would keep my odds of survival at precisely 50 per cent. However, if I place one white marble in one jar, and the other 99 marbles in the other, my chances go up to 1/2*1 + 1/2*49/99, or 74 per cent. This is as good as it gets. Still not a chance I'd take willingly without significant duress, but a lot better than 50 per cent!

TERMINUS

The victim's jumper was back to front as well as inside out. One would only have seen the label if standing in front of the man. Bligh claims to have seen the label as the victim ran away, which is impossible, and marks him as the killer.

THE FINAL CAMOUFLAGE

The theme was colour, and the words were *ash*, *bole*, *ceil* and *red*. I was stuck on a theme relating to trees for a long time.

SEVEN APPLEWOMEN

One pricing scheme is seven apples per penny, until less than seven remain, at which point the apples become three pence per apple. The fact that there are seven women with a maximum number of 140 apples ought to point you towards the divisive break. So the first woman gets two pence from 14 apples, plus 18 pence from her remaining six, whilst the last gets $140/7 = 20$ pence all from batches of seven apples per penny. The general solution for this sort of puzzle says that for x people with amounts of produce equal to $y(x + 0z) + x - 1, y(x + 1z) + x - 2, y(x + 2z) + x - 3$, ..., then these can be sold at x for one penny and then z for each remaining odd item, and all will receive $y + z(x - 1)$ pennies. In our case, y, an indeterminate factor in the equation, is equal to two, giving us a z of three for the x of seven.

ALSO AVAILABLE

Sherlock Holmes'
Elementary Puzzles
978-1-78097-578-8

Sherlock Holmes'
Fiendish Puzzles
978-1-78097-807-9

Sherlock Holmes'
Rudimentary Puzzles
978-1-78097-963-2